3 MINUTE SPANISH

LESSONS 7 – 9

KIERAN BALL

Copyright © 2019 Kieran Ball

All rights reserved.

Mother dearest...

I'd like to dedicate this book to my mum, who has given me so much in life, as well as life itself.

Thank you for your unequalled support, and thank you for being the one person in the world who has always held unwavering belief in everything I do.

You're the hardest working person I know and you have pushed me to be the greatest version of myself that I can be.

Hola y bienvenido (hello and welcome) to "3 Minute Spanish" . I'm Kieran and I'm a language tutor based in the UK and I wrote this book to help you to learn to speak Spanish.

The lessons in this book lead on from the last book "3 Minute Spanish: Lessons 4-6". The methodology will get you speaking quickly, without the struggle normally associated with language learning.

I'll not bore you with my life story or intricate details of the history of the methodology; I know you probably just want to start learning Spanish now, so I'll let you get on with it.

Actually, I've changed my mind, I will bore you a little before we start. It's my book! I'll keep it as brief as I can though.

I've been tutoring people for over ten years on a one-to-one basis in a range of subjects. I love languages, I love learning and I love teaching. I also love chocolate, but this isn't really the place to discuss my chocoholism. I'm very lucky that I get to teach people every day. However, I can't fit everybody who asks me into my schedule so, regrettably, I end up turning a lot of people away. I wish I could teach the whole world but I'm yet to figure out a way of duplicating myself!

The next best thing is to teach through the medium of a book. So, that's what I've decided to do. If you're reading this book, then I will soon be teaching you the glorious splendour that is the Spanish language.

Anyway, I'll stop blathering on in a minute and we'll get started with learning. But, firstly, let me just say this...

Hullabaloo!

No, I'm joking, of course, let me say this instead...

We are all human beings, which means we all possess the attributes that make us human beings. There's a wonderful quote by a man called Terence:

"I am human, and nothing that is human is alien to me"

What it means is that if one person is capable of something, then we are all capable of it, because we're all humans too. There's nothing in the world that I cannot understand if somebody before me has succeeded in understanding it. Therefore, it's only logical that since there are more than 500 million people in the world who have managed to learn to speak Spanish, then you can learn it too!

Anyway, philosophising over. Let's begin.

Contents

LESSON 7 6

LESSON 8 47

LESSON 9 101

Los números (*the numbers*) 129

Gracias 134

Visit my website or follow me on Facebook, Twitter
or Instagram for more language hints and tips:
www.3minute.club/udemy
www.twitter.com/3mlanguages
www.facebook.com/3minutelanguages
www.instagram.com/3minutelanguages

LESSON 7

Let's start this lesson with a quick recap of the words and phrases we learnt in the last lesson. How do you say the following in Spanish?

my
the hotel
nice
everybody / everyone

If there are any words you can't remember, go back to the last lesson and have a quick review of them before you start this lesson. It's really important that you remember the words you've learnt so far before you move on to learn any more.

Here's your first word for this lesson:

un

It means "a"
You pronounce it "oon"

The Spanish A

So far, we've seen that the Spanish have two words for "the":

el / la

Well, in Spanish, there are also two words for "a":

un / una
"a" (masculine / feminine)

You pronounce "un" as "oon".

You pronounce "una" as "oonah".

How would you say these three things in Spanish?

A chicken.

A pizza.

A restaurant.

A chicken.
Un pollo.

A pizza.
Una pizza.

A restaurant.
Un restaurante.

Here's a useful word if you ever find yourself thirsty in Spain:

un café

It means "a coffee"
You pronounce it "oon cah-FEH"

WORD LIST SO FAR

un / una – *a*
un café – *a coffee*

How would you say the following in Spanish?

A coffee for me.

The coffee here is delicious.

My coffee is terrible.

A coffee for me.
Un café para mí.

The coffee here is delicious.
El café aquí es delicioso.

My coffee is terrible.
Mi café es terrible.

If you don't really like coffee, perhaps this word might take your fancy:

un té

It means "a tea"
You pronounce it "oon TEH"

WORD LIST SO FAR

un / una – *a*
un café – *a coffee*
un té – *a tea*

How would you say the three sentences below in Spanish?

A tea for me.

The tea here is terrible.

My tea is absolutely delicious.

A tea for me.
Un té para mí.

The tea here is terrible.
El té aquí es terrible.

My tea is absolutely delicious.
Mi té es absolutamente delicioso.

We learnt previously that the word "gracias" means "thank you" in Spanish. Well, manners cost nothing, so here's another phrase:

por favor

It means "please"
You pronounce it "poor fah-VOR"

WORD LIST SO FAR

un / una – *a*
un café – *a coffee*
un té – *a tea*
por favor – *please*

How would you say these four sentences in Spanish?

A tea for me, please.

A coffee for him, please.

The pizza for me, please.

The chicken for her, please.

A tea for me, please.
Un té para mí, por favor.

A coffee for him, please.
Un café para él, por favor.

The pizza for me, please.
La pizza para mí, por favor.

The chicken for her, please.
El pollo para ella, por favor.

Here's an extremely useful word in Spanish:

quiero

It means "I would like"
You pronounce it "key-AIR-oh"

WORD LIST SO FAR

un / una – *a*
un café – *a coffee*
un té – *a tea*
por favor – *please*
quiero – *I would like*

How would you say the four sentences below in Spanish?

I would like a coffee, please.

I would like a tea for me.

I would like the chicken, please.

I would like the pizza.

I would like a coffee, please.
Quiero un café, por favor.

I would like a tea for me.
Quiero un té para mí.

I would like the chicken, please.
Quiero el pollo, por favor.

I would like the pizza.
Quiero la pizza.

Here's your next Spanish word:

una reserva

It means "a reservation"
You pronounce it "oona reh-SAIR-vah"

WORD LIST SO FAR

un / una – *a*
un café – *a coffee*
un té – *a tea*
por favor – *please*
quiero – *I would like*
una reserva – *a reservation*

How would you say these two sentences in Spanish?

I would like a reservation.

I would like a reservation, please.

I would like a reservation.
Quiero una reserva.

I would like a reservation, please.
Quiero una reserva, por favor.

Now, if you don't want to dine alone, you might want a reservation for:

dos personas

It means "two people"
You pronounce it "dos pair-SOH-nas"

WORD LIST SO FAR

un / una – *a*
un café – *a coffee*
un té – *a tea*
por favor – *please*
quiero – *I would like*
una reserva – *a reservation*
dos personas – *two people*

How would you say the four sentences below in Spanish?

I would like a reservation for two people, please.

It's for two people.

It's perfect for two people.

It isn't very good for two people.

I would like a reservation for two people, please.
Quiero una reserva para dos personas, por favor.

It's for two people.
Es para dos personas.

It's perfect for two people.
Es perfecto para dos personas.

It isn't very good for two people.
No es muy bueno para dos personas.

Here's your next word in Spanish:

una mesa

It means "a table"
You pronounce it "oona MESS-ah"

WORD LIST SO FAR

un / una – *a*
un café – *a coffee*
un té – *a tea*
por favor – *please*
quiero – *I would like*
una reserva – *a reservation*
dos personas – *two people*
una mesa – *a table*

How would you say these five sentences in Spanish?

I would like a table.

I would like a table, please.

I would like a table for two people, please.

A table for two, please.

I would like a table for three.

I would like a table.
Quiero una mesa.

I would like a table, please.
Quiero una mesa, por favor.

I would like a table for two people, please.
Quiero una mesa para dos personas, por favor.

A table for two, please.
Una mesa para dos, por favor.

I would like a table for three.
Quiero una mesa para tres.

A table for fifty!

Remember how I put a Vocabulary Expansion Section at the end of the last book. It had food and drink related vocabulary.

Well, I've put another Vocabulary Expansion Section at the end of this book for you, too. This time, it includes all the numbers in Spanish from zero to a thousand.

If you try and learn one to twelve off by heart, you will be able to get by in most situations.

It's time to practise what we've learnt in this lesson. How do you say these sentences in English?

1. The pizza for him, please
2. A table for two, please
3. A tea for him
4. I would like a reservation for two people, please
5. I would like a table for three people, please
6. A coffee for me
7. I would like the chicken, please
8. I would like a table for five people, please
9. I would like a coffee, please
10. I would like a tea, please

1. La pizza para él, por favor
2. Una mesa para dos, por favor
3. Un té para él
4. Quiero una reserva para dos personas, por favor
5. Quiero una mesa para tres personas, por favor
6. Un café para mí
7. Quiero el pollo, por favor
8. Quiero una mesa para cinco personas, por favor
9. Quiero un café, por favor
10. Quiero un té, por favor

Now, let's have a go at doing some reverse translations.

1. Una mesa para cinco personas, por favor
2. La pizza para él, por favor
3. Mi té es absolutamente terrible
4. Quiero una reserva, por favor
5. Una mesa para dos, por favor
6. Mi café es muy bueno
7. Quiero una mesa para ocho personas, por favor
8. Mi café es terrible
9. Quiero el pollo, por favor
10. Quiero una reserva para dos

1. **A table for five people, please**
2. **The pizza for him, please**
3. **My tea is absolutely terrible**
4. **I would like a reservation, please**
5. **A table for two, please**
6. **My coffee is very good**
7. **I would like a table for eight people, please**
8. **My coffee is terrible**
9. **I would like the chicken, please**
10. **I would like a reservation for two**

What we're going to do now are some recap translations, which will incorporate words we learnt in the previous lessons.

1. It's absolutely beautiful
2. I think the restaurant is fantastic
3. My chicken is terrible
4. It's absolutely delicious
5. The chicken is very good
6. I think it's delicious
7. I think everybody is very nice
8. It's perfect here
9. Everything is nice here
10. I think everything is perfect

1. Es absolutamente precioso
2. Para mí, el restaurante es fantástico
3. Mi pollo es terrible
4. Es absolutamente delicioso
5. El pollo es muy bueno
6. Para mí, es delicioso
7. Para mí, todo el mundo es muy simpático
8. Es perfecto aquí
9. Todo es simpático aquí
10. Para mí, todo es perfecto

Let's now do some Spanish to English recap translations.

1. Sí, es absolutamente delicioso
2. Es siempre muy bueno aquí
3. Para mí, es absolutamente precioso aquí
4. La pizza es para ella
5. Todo el mundo es simpático aquí
6. No es bueno aquí; es absolutamente fantástico
7. Mi hotel es precioso
8. Todo es terrible aquí
9. Es absolutamente precioso
10. Para mí, es muy bueno aquí

1. Yes, it's absolutely delicious
2. It's always very good here
3. I think it's absolutely beautiful here
4. The pizza is for her
5. Everybody is nice here
6. It isn't good here; it's absolutely fantastic
7. My hotel is beautiful
8. Everything is terrible here
9. It's absolutely beautiful
10. I think it's very good here

Let's recap all the words we've learnt so far. How did you say these words in Spanish?

1. for him
2. no
3. the chicken
4. a coffee
5. perfect
6. the restaurant
7. always
8. extraordinary
9. fantastic
10. it isn't
11. yes
12. nice
13. here
14. the pizza
15. very
16. two people
17. delicious
18. a table
19. beautiful
20. everything
21. a tea
22. for her
23. everybody
24. is
25. it is
26. thank you
27. the hotel
28. I think
29. for me
30. a
31. terrible
32. a reservation
33. but
34. my
35. I would like
36. absolutely
37. please
38. good
39. isn't
40. that
41. that is...

1. para él
2. no
3. el pollo
4. un café
5. perfecto
6. el restaurante
7. siempre
8. extraordinario
9. fantástico
10. no es
11. sí
12. simpático
13. aquí
14. la pizza
15. muy
16. dos personas
17. delicioso
18. una mesa
19. precioso
20. todo
21. un té
22. para ella
23. todo el mundo
24. es
25. es
26. gracias
27. el hotel
28. para mí
29. para mí
30. un
31. terrible
32. una reserva
33. pero
34. mi
35. quiero
36. absolutamente
37. por favor
38. bueno
39. no es
40. eso
41. eso es...

LESSON 8

Let's start this lesson with a quick recap of the words and phrases we learnt in the last lesson. How do you say the following in Spanish?

>a (masculine / feminine)
>a tea
>a table
>I would like
>two people
>please
>a coffee
>a reservation

If there are any words you can't remember, go back to the last lesson and have a quick review of them before you start this lesson. It's really important that you remember the words you've learnt so far before you move on to learn any more.

Here's your first word for this lesson:

la comida

It means "the food"
You pronounce it "lah coh-MEE-dah"

How would you say these three sentences in Spanish?

The food is here.

The food is delicious.

The food here is always very good.

The food is here.
La comida es buena aquí.

The food is delicious.
La comida es deliciosa.

The food here is always very good.
La comida aquí es siempre buena.

Here's a useful little linking word in Spanish:

y

It means "and"
You pronounce it "eee"

WORD LIST SO FAR

la comida – *the food*
y – *and*

How would you say the three sentences below in Spanish?

I would like a tea and a coffee.

I would like the chicken for me and the pizza for him.

María and Pedro.

I would like a tea and a coffee.
Quiero un té y un café.

I would like the chicken for me and the pizza for him.
Quiero el pollo para mí y la pizza para él.

María and Pedro.
María y Pedro.

This is a nice little word:

también

It means "also"
You pronounce it "tam-bee-EN"

WORD LIST SO FAR

la comida – *the food*
y – *and*
también – *also*

How would you say these two sentences in Spanish?

I would like a tea and also a coffee.

Also, I would like a coffee for me, please.

I would like a tea and also a coffee.
Quiero un té y también un café.

Also, I would like a coffee for me, please.
También, quiero un café para mí, por favor.

The word for "is" in Spanish is "es". Here's another useful word:

son

It means "are"
You pronounce it "son"

WORD LIST SO FAR

la comida – *the food*
y – *and*
también – *also*
son – *are*

How would you say the following four sentences in Spanish?

The tea and the coffee are for me.

That and that are for him.

The pizza and the chicken are for me.

The tea and the coffee are for me.

The tea and the coffee are for me.
El té y el café son para mí.

That and that are for him.
Eso y eso son para él.

The pizza and the chicken are for me.
La pizza y el pollo son para mí.

The tea and the coffee are for me.
El té y el café son para mí.

The opposite to "son", in Spanish, is:

no son

It means "are not"
You pronounce it "noh son"

WORD LIST SO FAR

la comida – *the food*
y – *and*
también – *also*
son – *are*
no son – *aren't*

How would you say this in Spanish?

The tea and the coffee aren't for him.

The tea and the coffee aren't for him.
El té y el café no son para él.

The Spanish THE

So far, we've seen that the Spanish have two words for "the":

EL & LA

Well, there is actually a third and fourth way:

LOS & LAS

These are used when there is more than one of something. You use LOS in front of masculine nouns and LAS in front of feminine nouns.

E.g. las mesas = the tables
los pollos = the chickens

We call them the "plural the"

el
the (masculine singular)

la
the (feminine singular)

los
the (masculine plural)

las
the (feminine plural)

The Spanish plural

In English, most of the time, if you want to make a noun plural, you just add an 's' to the end. E.g. "chicken" becomes "chickens" in the plural.

Most of the time, you can do this in Spanish, too. You just put an 's' on the end of the noun and put the "plural the" in front of it. Look at the examples below:

el pollo – los pollos
the chicken – the chickens

la pizza – las pizzas
the pizza – the pizzas

el restaurante – los restaurantes
the restaurant – the restaurants

Here is a list of singular nouns. See if you can make them plural. I've put the answers on the next page:

1. el pollo (the chicken)
2. la pizza (the pizza)
3. el restaurante (the restaurant)
4. el hotel (the hotel)
5. el café (the coffee)
6. el té (the tea)
7. la mesa (the table)
8. la persona (the person)
9. la reserva (the reservation)
10. la llave (the key)
11. el libro (the book)
12. la casa (the house)
13. el vino (the wine)
14. el vaso (the glass)

Here are the answers. I hope you got them all right!

1. los pollos (the chickens)
2. las pizzas (the pizzas)
3. los restaurantes (the restaurants)
4. los hoteles* (the hotels)
5. los cafés (the coffees)
6. los tés (the teas)
7. las mesas (the tables)
8. las personas (the people)
9. las reservas (the reservations)
10. las llaves (the keys)
11. los libros (the books)
12. las casas (the houses)
13. los vinos (the wines)
14. los vasos (the glasses)

*when a word ends in a consonant, to make it plural you have to add –es. Therefore, "el hotel" becomes "los hoteles".

WORD LIST SO FAR

la comida – *the food*
y – *and*
también – *also*
son – *are*
no son – *aren't*
los / las – *the (masculine plural / feminine plural)*

How would you say these two sentences in Spanish?

The coffees are for her.

The restaurants.

The coffees are for her.
Los cafés son para ella.

The restaurants.
Los restaurantes.

Making the adjective agree

Remember, I showed you that all adjectives have a feminine form that you have to use when talking about a feminine noun?

Well, there are also plural forms. You use these to talk about plural nouns.

So, that means each adjective in Spanish has four different forms. I'll show you with the adjective "bueno" (good).

el pollo es <u>**bueno**</u>
the chicken is good (masculine singular)

la pizza es <u>buena</u>
the pizza is good (feminine singular)

los pollos son <u>**buenos**</u>
the chickens are good (masculine plural)

las pizzas son <u>buenas</u>
the pizzas are good (feminine plural)

Every single adjective has these four forms. I've laid out all the different forms of each of the adjectives we've learnt so far.

It goes "***English*** – masculine singular – masculine plural – feminine singular – feminine plural".

GOOD – BUENO – BUENOS – BUENA – BUENAS

DELICIOUS – DELICIOSO – DELICIOSOS – DELICIOSA – DELICIOSAS

FANTASTIC – FANTÁSTICO – FANTÁSTICOS – FANTÁSTICA – FANTÁSTICAS

BEAUTIFUL – PRECIOSO – PRECIOSOS – PRECIOSA – PRECIOSAS

EXTRAORDINARY – EXTRAORDINARIO – EXTRAORDINARIOS – EXTRAORDINARIA – EXTRAORDINARIAS

PERFECT – PERFECTO – PERFECTOS – PERFECTA – PERFECTAS

BAD – MALO – MALOS – MALA – MALAS

TERRIBLE – TERRIBLE – TERRIBLES – TERRIBLE – TERRIBLES

NICE – SIMPÁTICO – SIMPÁTICOS – SIMPÁTICA - SIMPÁTICAS

You'll probably see a pattern. If an adjective ends in an 'o', the 'o' becomes an 'os' in the masculine plural, an 'a' in the feminine, and an 'as' in the feminine plural. If a word ends in an 'e', like "terrible", then you just add an 's' in both the plurals, and it stays the same in the feminine.

Masculine or Feminine?

So, when you're talking about masculine nouns you use the masculine singular or the masculine plural versions of the adjective, and when you're talking about a feminine noun you use the feminine singular or the feminine plural versions of the adjectives.

el pollo es **bueno**

los pollos son **buenos**

la pizza es **buena**

las pizzas son **buenas**

However, what if you want to say something like this?

The chicken and the pizza are good

Well, whenever you're talking about a mixture of masculine and feminine nouns, the masculine plural adjective is always used.

El pollo y la pizza son **buenos**

Now, let's practise a little with these adjective agreement rules. Here's a random feminine noun:

una zanahoria

It means "a carrot"
You pronounce it "oonah sah-nah-OH-ree-ah"

WORD LIST SO FAR

la comida – *the food*
y – *and*
también – *also*
son – *are*
no son – *aren't*
los / las – *the (masculine plural / feminine plural)*
una zanahoria – *a carrot*

How would you say these three things in Spanish?

The carrot.

The carrots.

The carrots are good.

The carrot.
La zanahoria.

The carrots.
Las zanahorias.

The carrots are good.
Las zanahorias son buenas.

And here's a random masculine noun:

un plátano

It means "a banana"
You pronounce it "oon PLAH-tah-noh"

WORD LIST SO FAR

la comida – *the food*
y – *and*
también – *also*
son – *are*
no son – *aren't*
los / las – *the (masculine plural / feminine plural)*
una zanahoria – *a carrot*
un plátano – *a banana*

How would you say the three things below in Spanish?

The banana.

The bananas.

The bananas are good.

The banana.
El plátano.

The bananas.
Los plátanos.

The bananas are good.
Los plátanos son buenos.

The Spanish MY

We've seen the first version of "my" in Spanish. Well, there's a plural version too:

mi
my (singular)

mis
my (plural)

WORD LIST SO FAR

la comida – *the food*
y – *and*
también – *also*
son – *are*
no son – *aren't*
los / las – *the (masculine plural / feminine plural)*
una zanahoria – *a carrot*
un plátano – *a banana*
mis – *my (plural)*

How would you say the following two sentences in Spanish?

My carrots are delicious.

My bananas are delicious.

My carrots are delicious.
Mis zanahorias son deliciosas.

My bananas are delicious.
Mis plátanos son deliciosos.

Quick test

Let's do a quick test. See if you can translate these sentences into Spanish. The answers are on the next page.

1. My chicken is good.
2. My pizza is good.
3. My bananas are good.
4. My carrots are good.
5. The chicken here is good.
6. The pizza here is good.
7. The bananas here are good.
8. The carrots here are good.

Answers

1. Mi pollo es bueno.
2. Mi pizza es buena.
3. Mis plátanos son buenos.
4. Mis zanahorias son buenas.
5. El pollo aquí es bueno.
6. La pizza aquí es buena.
7. Los plátanos aquí son buenos.
8. Las zanahorias aquí son buenas.

Don't lose sleep

This lesson has been full of little grammar rules. They aren't difficult to understand but there are a lot to remember

However, I always say, "Don't lose sleep!" I've introduced these grammatical structures very early on in the course but I don't expect you to remember them all whenever you speak Spanish. The reason I've introduced them now is because it's best to get them out of the way with early, and then the more you see them, the more you'll remember them.

The most important thing when speaking a foreign language is just making sure you're understood. Whether you miss off a letter or use the wrong word for "the", as long as you're speaking and the other person understands what you're saying, it doesn't matter in the slightest.

Worrying about these rules will only stop you from wanting to speak but at the same time, knowing about them will make it easier in the long run. But, as I said, don't lose sleep over them. Even the most fluent of speakers makes a slip-up with these rules now and again so just learn them and then focus on the speaking.

It's time to practise what we've learnt in this lesson.

1. The food here is always delicious
2. I would like two chickens, please, one for me and one for her
3. The carrots are very good
4. I think the food is perfect here
5. The bananas are very good
6. The food is always terrible
7. The chicken for me and the pizza for her, please
8. The food here is very good
9. The chicken is delicious
10. The pizza and the chicken are very good

1. La comida aquí es siempre deliciosa
2. Quiero dos pollos, por favor, un para mí y un para ella
3. Las zanahorias son muy buenas
4. Para mí, la comida es perfecta aquí
5. Los plátanos son muy buenos
6. La comida es siempre terrible
7. El pollo para mí y la pizza para ella, por favor
8. La comida aquí es muy buena
9. El pollo es delicioso
10. La pizza y el pollo son muy buenos

Now, let's have a go at doing some reverse translations.

1. La comida aquí es muy buena
2. La pizza es deliciosa
3. Mi comida es deliciosa
4. Las zanahorias son terribles
5. El pollo es delicioso
6. Los plátanos son muy buenos
7. Quiero dos tés y tres cafés
8. Quiero un té para él y un café para ella
9. También, quiero un café, por favor
10. Mis zanahorias son perfectas

1. **The food here is very good**
2. **The pizza is delicious**
3. **My food is delicious**
4. **The carrots are terrible**
5. **The chicken is delicious**
6. **The bananas are very good**
7. **I would like two teas and three coffees**
8. **I would like a tea for him and a coffee for her**
9. **Also, I would like a coffee, please**
10. **My carrots are perfect**

What we're going to do now are some recap translations, which will incorporate words we learnt in the previous lessons.

1. It isn't very good
2. I would like a coffee, please
3. Everybody is very nice
4. The restaurant is very good
5. The hotel is terrible
6. It's good
7. The chicken is very good
8. The pizza is very good
9. It isn't very delicious
10. I would like a tea for him, please

1. **No es muy bueno**
2. **Quiero un café, por favor**
3. **Todo el mundo es muy simpático**
4. **El restaurante es muy bueno**
5. **El hotel es terrible**
6. **Es bueno**
7. **El pollo es muy bueno**
8. **La pizza es muy buena**
9. **No es muy delicioso**
10. **Quiero un té para él, por favor**

Let's now do some Spanish to English recap translations.

1. Eso es delicioso pero no es muy bueno para mí
2. No es fantástico pero es muy bueno
3. No para ella
4. El restaurante no es malo
5. No es para ella ; es para él
6. No es para él ; es para mí
7. El pollo es muy bueno pero la pizza es extraordinaria
8. Para mí, la pizza es extraordinaria
9. Eso para mí, gracias
10. Es muy bueno

1. That is delicious but it isn't very good for me
2. It isn't fantastic but it's very good
3. Not for her
4. The restaurant isn't bad
5. It isn't for her; it's for him
6. It isn't for him; it's for me
7. The chicken is very good but the pizza is extraordinary
8. I think the pizza is extraordinary
9. That for me, thank you
10. It's very good

Let's recap all the words we've learnt so far. How did you say these words in Spanish?

1. nice
2. my
3. everything
4. for me
5. a coffee
6. a carrot
7. it is
8. please
9. the restaurant
10. the pizza
11. I think
12. that is…
13. but
14. and
15. for her
16. yes
17. a banana
18. perfect
19. I would like
20. the (plural)
21. the food
22. aren't
23. no
24. a
25. very
26. a table
27. everybody
28. always
29. also
30. here
31. beautiful
32. my (plural)
33. a reservation
34. that
35. good
36. isn't
37. extraordinary
38. a tea
39. it isn't
40. absolutely
41. delicious
42. the chicken
43. the hotel
44. are
45. fantastic
46. terrible

47. thank you
48. is
49. for him
50. two people

1. simpático
2. mi
3. todo
4. para mí
5. un café
6. una zanahoria
7. es
8. por favor
9. el restaurante
10. la pizza
11. para mí
12. eso es...
13. pero
14. y
15. para ella
16. sí
17. un plátano
18. perfecto
19. quiero
20. los / las
21. la comida
22. no son
23. no
24. un / una
25. muy
26. una mesa
27. todo el mundo
28. siempre
29. también
30. aquí
31. precioso
32. mis
33. una reserva
34. eso
35. bueno
36. no es
37. extraordinario
38. un té
39. no es
40. absolutamente
41. delicioso
42. el pollo
43. el hotel
44. son
45. fantástico
46. terrible
47. gracias
48. es
49. para él
50. dos personas

LESSON 9

Let's start this lesson with a quick recap of the words and phrases we learnt in the last lesson. How do you say the following in Spanish?

a banana
the (plural)
my (plural)
aren't
a carrot
and
the food
are
also

If there are any words you can't remember, go back to the last lesson and have a quick review of them before you start this lesson. It's really important that you remember the words you've learnt so far before you move on to learn any more.

Now the previous lesson was rather intense, what with all the masculine, feminine, singular and plural rules. Therefore, I'm going to make this lesson a little less taxing. I'll call it the "Greetings Lesson", and you'll soon see why.

Here's your first word for this lesson:

hola

It means "hello"
You pronounce it "OH-lah"

How would you say these three sentences in Spanish?

Hello, I'd like a coffee, please.

Hello, a tea for me, please.

Hello, the pizza for me and the chicken for him, please.

Hello, I'd like a coffee, please.
Hola, quiero un café, por favor.

Hello, a tea for me, please.
Hola, un té para mí, por favor.

Hello, the pizza for me and the chicken for him, please.
Hola, la pizza para mí y el pollo para él, por favor.

Here's your next greetings based word:

buenos días

It means "good day" or "good morning"
You pronounce it "bwe-nos DEE-ass"

WORD LIST SO FAR

hola – *hello*
buenos días *–good day / good morning*

How would you say the three things below in Spanish?

Good day, two coffees, please.

Good day, I'd like a table for two, please.

Good morning.

Good day, two coffees, please.
Buenos días, dos cafés, por favor.

Good day, I'd like a table for two, please.
Buenos días, quiero una mesa para dos, por favor.

Good morning.
Buenos días.

This is a nice little word:

buenas tardes

It means "good afternoon" or "good evening"
You pronounce it "bweh-nass TAR-dess"

WORD LIST SO FAR

hola – *hello*
buenos días *–good day / good morning*
buenas tardes – *good afternoon / good evening*

How would you say these three sentences in Spanish?

Good evening, I'd like a table for three people, please.

Good afternoon, two teas, please.

Good evening, I would like a pizza, please.

Good evening, I'd like a table for three people, please.
Buenas tardes, quiero una mesa para tres personas, por favor.

Good afternoon, two teas, please.
Buenas tardes, dos tés, por favor.

Good evening, I would like a pizza, please.
Buenas tardes, quiero una pizza, por favor.

Here's your next word in Spanish:

buenas noches

It means "goodnight"
You pronounce it "bweh-nas NOH-chess"

Here's another word that goes nicely with the last word:

adiós

It means "goodbye"
You pronounce it "ah-dee-OSS"

How would you say this in Spanish?

Goodbye and goodnight.

Goodbye and goodnight.
Adiós y buenas noches.

Here's a final greetings phrase in Spanish:

hasta luego

It means "see you soon"
You pronounce it "ass-tah LWEH-goh"

WORD LIST SO FAR

hola – *hello*
buenos días – *good morning / good day*
buenas tardes – *good afternoon / good evening*
buenas noches – *goodnight*
adiós – *goodbye*
hasta luego – *see you soon*

How would you say these two sentences in Spanish?

See you soon.

Goodbye and see you soon.

See you soon.
Hasta luego.

Goodbye and see you soon.
Adiós y hasta luego.

Quick test

Let's just have a quick test.

See if you can remember what all of these are in Spanish (the answers are on the next page):

1. Hello
2. Good day
3. Good evening
4. Goodnight
5. Good afternoon
6. Good morning
7. Goodbye
8. See you soon

Answers

1. Hola
2. Buenos días
3. Buenas tardes
4. Buenas noches
5. Buenas tardes
6. Buenos días
7. Adiós
8. Hasta luego

It's time to practise what we've learnt in this lesson.

1. Goodbye and see you soon
2. Hello, I'd like two teas, please
3. Good day
4. Goodnight
5. Hello
6. Good evening
7. Goodbye
8. Hello, I'd like a coffee, please
9. Good morning
10. See you soon

1. **Adiós y hasta luego**
2. **Hola, quiero dos tés, por favor**
3. **Buenos días**
4. **Buenas noches**
5. **Hola**
6. **Buenas tardes**
7. **Adiós**
8. **Hola, quiero un café, por favor**
9. **Buenos días**
10. **Hasta luego**

Now, let's have a go at doing some reverse translations.

1. Buenas tardes
2. Adiós
3. Buenos días
4. Hola
5. Buenas noches
6. Adiós y buenas noches
7. Hola, quiero dos tés y un café
8. Buenas tardes, quiero un café, por favor
9. Buenas tardes, quiero una mesa para dos, por favor
10. Hasta luego

1. Good evening
2. Goodbye
3. Good day
4. Hello
5. Goodnight
6. Goodbye and goodnight
7. Hello, I'd like two teas and a coffee
8. Good evening, I would like a coffee, please
9. Good evening, I would like a table for two, please
10. See you soon

What we're going to do now are some recap translations, which will incorporate words we learnt in the previous lessons.

1. I think that is absolutely extraordinary
2. The food is fantastic
3. It's extraordinary here
4. Also, I'd like a coffee, please
5. Everything here is delicious
6. The food is always delicious here
7. That is for me
8. I would like a table for three people
9. It's for her
10. Everything is fantastic here

1. Para mí, eso es absolutamente extraordinario
2. La comida es fantástica
3. Es extraordinario aquí
4. También, quiero un café, por favor
5. Todo aquí es delicioso
6. La comida es siempre deliciosa aquí
7. Eso es para mí
8. Quiero una mesa para tres personas
9. Es para ella
10. Todo es fantástico aquí

Let's now do some Spanish to English recap translations.

1. No es muy bueno para mí
2. Sí, es para mí
3. Eso no es muy bueno para mí
4. Quiero un café, por favor
5. No es para ella; es para mí
6. La comida es terrible
7. El pollo es delicioso
8. No es malo aquí
9. Todo el mundo es muy simpático
10. Quiero una mesa para cinco, por favor

1. It isn't very good for me
2. Yes, it's for me
3. That isn't very good for me
4. I would like a coffee, please
5. It isn't for her; it's for me
6. The food is terrible
7. The chicken is delicious
8. It isn't bad here
9. Everybody is very nice
10. I would like a table for five, please

Let's recap all the words we've learnt so far. How did you say these words in Spanish?

1. fantastic
2. everything
3. isn't
4. hello
5. delicious
6. also
7. here
8. a coffee
9. everybody
10. I think / in my opinion
11. that is
12. goodnight
13. it is
14. for her
15. perfect
16. and
17. is
18. two people
19. a
20. no
21. a table
22. see you later
23. good evening
24. nice
25. a banana
26. aren't
27. that
28. the chicken
29. terrible
30. the food
31. goodbye
32. the paella
33. the restaurant
34. good day
35. I would like
36. yes
37. a carrot
38. my (plural)
39. but
40. are
41. beautiful
42. the hotel
43. for him
44. a reservation
45. good

46. absolutely
47. very
48. bad
49. my
50. a tea
51. thank you
52. it isn't
53. always
54. please
55. the (plural)
56. for me
57. extraordinary

1. fantástico
2. todo
3. no es
4. hola
5. delicioso
6. también
7. aquí
8. un café
9. todo el mundo
10. para mí
11. eso es
12. buenas noches
13. es
14. para ella
15. perfecto
16. y
17. es
18. dos personas
19. un / una
20. no
21. una mesa
22. hasta luego
23. buenas tardes
24. simpático
25. un plátano
26. no son
27. eso
28. el pollo
29. terrible
30. la comida
31. adiós
32. la paella
33. el restaurante
34. buenos días
35. quiero
36. sí
37. una zanahoria
38. mis
39. pero
40. son
41. precioso
42. el hotel
43. para él
44. una reserva
45. bueno
46. absolutamente
47. muy
48. malo
49. mi
50. un té
51. gracias
52. no es
53. siempre
54. por favor
55. los/las
56. para mí
57. extraordinario

Vocabulary Expansion Section

los números
the numbers

0-10

0   cero
1   uno
2   dos
3   tres
4   cuatro
5   cinco
6   seis
7   siete
8   ocho
9   nueve
10 diez

11-20

11 once
12 doce
13 trece
14 catorce
15 quince
16 dieciséis
17 diecisiete
18 dieciocho
19 diecinueve
20 veinte

21-30

21 veintiuno
22 veintidós
23 veintitrés
24 veinticuatro
25 veinticinco
26 veintiséis
27 veintisiete
28 veintiocho
29 veintinueve
30 treinta

31-40

31 treinta y uno
32 treinta y dos
33 treinta y tres
34 treinta y cuatro
35 treinta y cinco
36 treinta y seis
37 treinta y siete
38 treinta y ocho
39 treinta y nueve
40 cuarenta

41-50

41 cuarenta y uno
42 cuarenta y dos
43 cuarenta y tres
44 cuarenta y cuatro
45 cuarenta y cinco
46 cuarenta y seis
47 cuarenta y siete
48 cuarenta y ocho
49 cuarenta y nueve
50 cincuenta

51-60

51 cincuenta y uno
52 cincuenta y dos
53 cincuenta y tres
54 cincuenta y cuatro
55 cincuenta y cinco
56 cincuenta y seis
57 cincuenta y siete
58 cincuenta y ocho
59 cincuenta y nueve
60 sesenta

61-70

61 sesenta y uno
62 sesenta y dos
63 sesenta y tres
64 sesenta y cuatro
65 sesenta y cinco
66 sesenta y seis
67 sesenta y siete
68 sesenta y ocho
69 sesenta y nueve
70 setenta

71-80

71 setenta y uno
72 setenta y dos
73 setenta y tres
74 setenta y cuatro
75 setenta y cinco
76 setenta y seis
77 setenta y siete
78 setenta y ocho
79 setenta y nueve
80 ochenta

81-90

81 ochenta y uno
82 ochenta y dos
83 ochenta y tres
84 ochenta y cuatro
85 ochenta y cinco
86 ochenta y seis
87 ochenta y siete
88 ochenta y ocho
89 ochenta y nueve
90 noventa

91-100

91 noventa y uno
92 noventa y dos
93 noventa y tres
94 noventa y cuatro
95 noventa y cinco
96 noventa y seis
97 noventa y siete
98 noventa y ocho
99 noventa y nueve
100 cien

101-110

101 ciento uno
102 ciento dos
103 ciento tres
104 ciento cuatro
105 ciento cinco
106 ciento seis
107 ciento siete
108 ciento ocho
109 ciento nueve
110 ciento diez

200-210

200 doscientos
201 doscientos uno
202 doscientos dos
203 doscientos tres
204 doscientos cuatro
205 doscientos cinco
206 doscientos seis
207 doscientos siete
208 doscientos ocho
209 doscientos nueve
210 doscientos diez

300-1000

300 trescientos
301 trescientos uno
302 trescientos dos
303 trescientos tres
400 cuatrocientos
500 quinientos
600 seiscientos
700 setecientos
800 ochocientos
900 novecientos
1000 mil
1000000 un millón

Gracias

Before you go, I'd like to say "gracias" for buying this book. There are lots of Spanish books available on Amazon and you chose to read mine, so I am eternally grateful for that.

I hope you have enjoyed this book and I hope you're glad you made the purchase. I also hope you've started to realise how easy learning a new language can be.

This book contained lessons seven to nine of my "3 Minute Spanish" course. If you would like to learn more, you can get the next book in the series containing lessons ten to twelve, and further books after that to continue building your Spanish language skills.

For more information on where to get the next books, or if you'd like any more tips on language learning, you can visit my website www.3minute.club/udemy

You can also follow me on Twitter, Facebook or Instagram:

www.twitter.com/3mlanguages

www.facebook.com/3minutelanguages

www.instagram.com/3minutelanguages

If you liked this book, you might also like my other language course series:

3 Minute Languages

The 3 Minute Languages courses are perfect for the complete beginner. They will get you speaking a language from scratch, assuming you know absolutely nothing. You will be amazed at how quickly you're able to put sentences together. And you will memorise new words and phrases easily without even trying.

Building Structures

The Building Structures courses are a revolutionary way to look at foreign language acquisition; you will learn how any language can be broken down into around fifteen structures. Each course focuses on a different structure, and you will learn how to form it, make it negative and turn it into a question. Each structure gives you a huge amount to say, and once you've learnt all fifteen structures, you will know everything about the language. All you have to do is fill in the gaps with words to form a sentence. These courses are for students who are slightly familiar with the language, and what to boost their progress.

Quick Guides

The Quick Guides are grammar guides. I recommend these for students who have already been learning the language, and would like to accelerate your learning. The Quick Guides are perfect for anybody who wants an in-depth look at a specific grammar point within the language.

You can get discounts on all of my courses on Udemy by using the discount code **3MINUTE** on checkout. Find the full list here: www.3minute.club/udemy

Thank you again, ¡gracias y hasta luego!

Printed in Poland
by Amazon Fulfillment
Poland Sp. z o.o., Wrocław